First Natu

The A...

Gunilla Ingves

A & C Black · London

A & C Black (Publishers) Ltd, 35 Bedford Row,
London WC1R 4JH
First published by Natur och Kultur, Sweden under the series title *Har du sett på...*

Translated by Jane Sutton
Nature advisor English text, Jean Imrie

Ingves, Gunilla
Ant. — (first nature books)
1. The Ant — Juvenile literature
I. Title II. Myran. *English*
III. Series
595.79'6 QL568.F7
ISBN 0-7136-2648-8

ISBN 0-7136-2648-8

This edition arranged with the help of Angus Hudson, London
Printed and bound in Great Britain by Purnell and Son (Book Production) Ltd., Paulton, Bristol

Look inside this anthill. There are lots of tunnels and rooms inside. Some of the tunnels go underground.

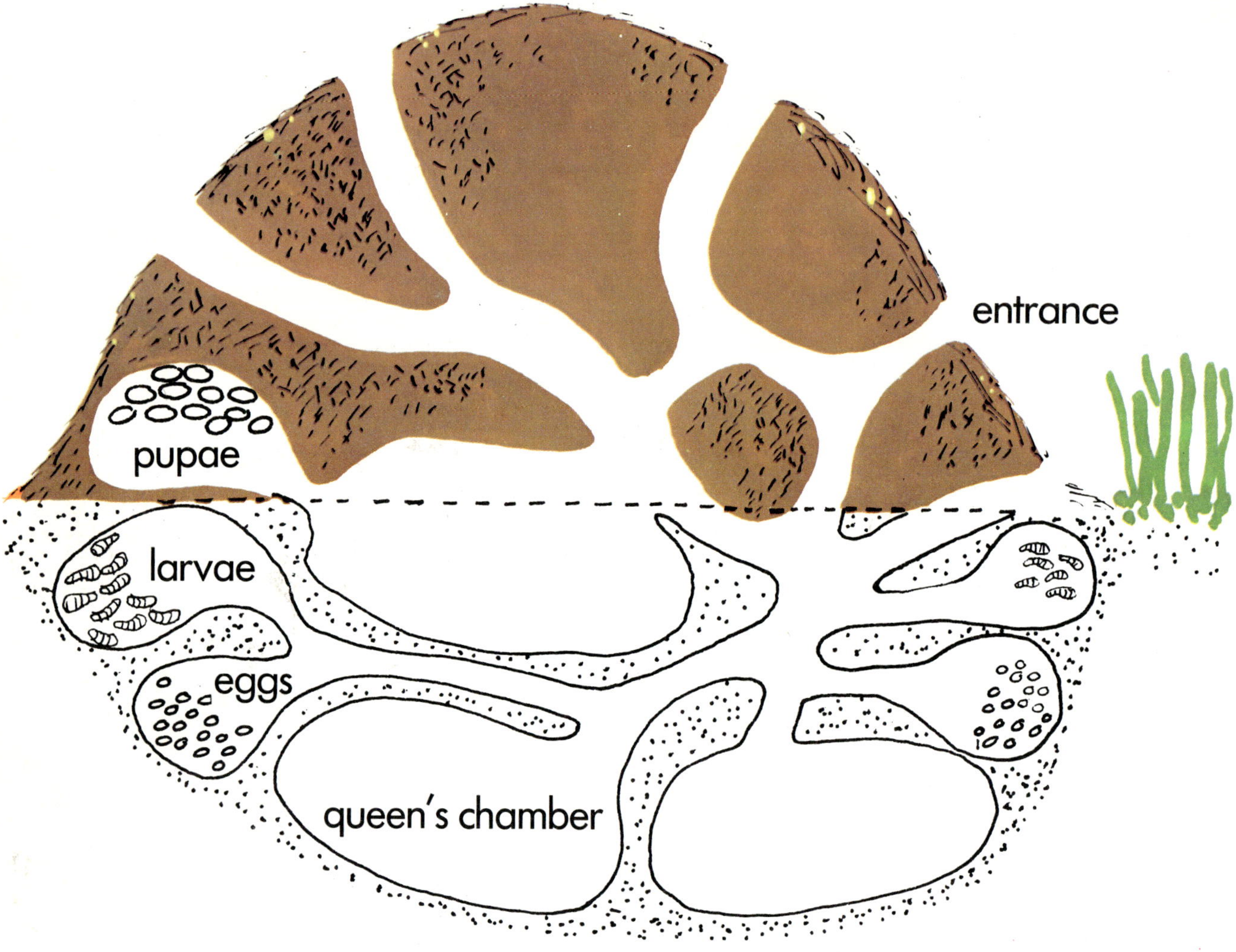

It is a warm, sunny day and lots of ants with wings are going outside. The big ants are female. They are called queens. The small ants are male ants.

When they get outside, the male ants and queen ants mate. Soon the queen ants will lay lots of eggs.

After they have mated, the male ants try to fly away. Some are eaten by a bird. The other ants fall down because they are weak. They soon die.

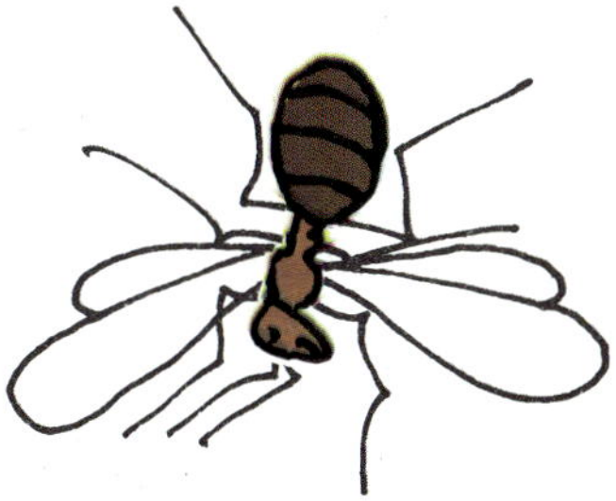

The queen ants are getting ready to lay their eggs. Each queen ant makes a nest and breaks off her wings. She doesn't need her wings any more because she won't leave her nest again.

In the nest, the queen lays some eggs which produce worker ants. Each worker ant has a special job to do. One worker ant is bringing food for the queen. Another worker ant keeps her clean.

The queen ant lays hundreds of eggs every day. Some worker ants move the eggs to a special room called the egg chamber. It is their job to look after the eggs. They lick the eggs to keep them clean.

Nine days later, it is time for the eggs to hatch. Out come fat, white larvae. The worker ants are busy feeding all the larvae.

They move the larvae to another room, called the larvae chamber. Another worker ant carries the empty egg shell outside to the rubbish dump.

The larvae eat and eat for a week until they are fully grown. They spin some sticky threads from their mouths, and wrap the threads around their bodies to make a cocoon.

Now the little insect is called a pupa. Inside the cocoon, it is changing from a larva into an ant. This takes twelve days. Then two worker ants open each cocoon with their jaws and help the young ant out.

It is a little worker ant. It is very weak and pale. The worker ants feed it and keep it clean. Soon the new ant grows strong and turns brown in colour.

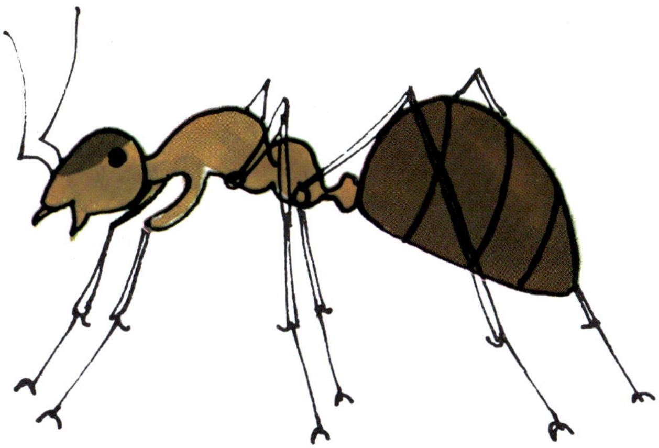

This is what the little worker ant looks like. On its head, there are two antennae. It uses these to feel and smell things. The ant has six legs.

The fat part of the ant's body is called abdomen. In the abdomen, there is a sac with poison in it. The ant squirts the poison at insects it wants to eat or at enemies.

male ant

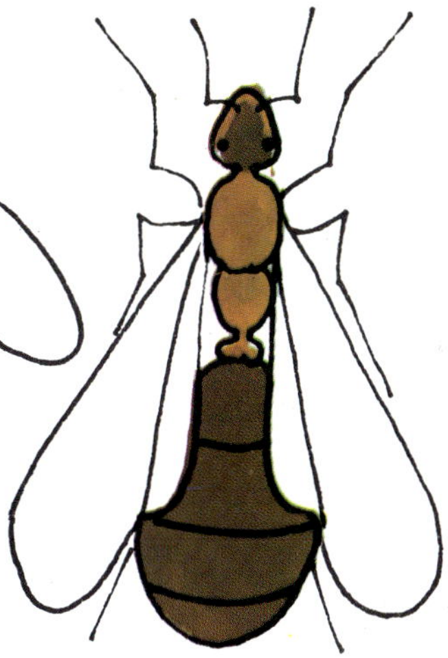

queen ant

Some of the new ants are males and some are queens. But most of the new ants are worker ants. Worker ants don't mate and don't lay eggs. Male ants and queen ants don't do any work. They rest until it is time to mate.

Outside the anthill, two worker ants meet. They put their antennae together to see if they know each other. One of the ants is full of food. It has left a trail for the other ant to follow. The trail leads to a plant where there are lots of greenfly.

The greenfly are making a juice called honeydew. The ant likes honeydew.
It holds the greenfly with its antennae and sucks the honeydew from the back of the greenfly. The ant stores some of the honeydew in its stomach to use later.

Along comes a ladybird. The ladybird likes to eat greenfly. The ant tries to bite the ladybird to make it stop. But the ladybird's shell is very hard.

The ant goes back to the anthill. It brings up some of the honeydew it has stored to feed the larvae.

In a tunnel, the ant meets a rose beetle larva. The ant wants to eat it. But the larva smells so horrid that the ant goes away.

Outside, the ant meets some other worker ants. They are busy mending the anthill. One carries a twig, one carries a pine needle and one carries a ball of gum.

Here comes a fox. He likes to eat ants and ant eggs. A soldier ant with big jaws bites the fox's nose. Another ant squirts its poison at the fox. The hungry fox goes away.

The ant goes off to find more food. It finds a dead weevil. But the ant can't move the weevil on its own. Another ant comes along to help.

The two ants drag and push the weevil back to the nest. They put it in the food store to use later.

An ant from another anthill is watching. It tries to get into the food store to take the weevil. But these three soldier ants can smell the ant. They can tell that it is not from their anthill. The soldiers drive the ant away.

At the end of the day, the ants close the entrances to the anthill with twigs and leaves. The soldier ants will keep watch for enemies while the other ants sleep.